This book is dedicated to my incredible son, who I am so proud of every day.

Harry's New Wings

Written By Claire Lamb

Illustrated by Emmie Schofield

Harry was a caterpillar,

green and black and happy,

spending his days eating leaves,

dreaming of the day he would be...

A butterfly, like those he saw,

flying high and proud,

showing off their colours,

to everyone around.

They danced and dipped gracefully,

landing from flower to flower,

Harry watched on contentedly,

as his pace turned a little slower,

knowing it wouldn't be long,

until his time would come,

to fly among the butterflies,

singing his own song.

Tiredness made Harry sleep,

he dreamed of butterflies,

of the colours he would show the world,

as he flew so very high.

What would he be?

Harry wanted to know,

would he be red? Black? Both?

Or maybe even blue,

Harry sighed happily as he closed his eyes,

not long now, he would find out soon.

Harry slept for a long time,

longer than he realised,

slowly he began to stretch,

and open up his eyes.

Harry felt different today,

much lighter than before,

he unfurled his brand-new wings

and he began to soar!

"Oh My!"

Harry cried.

"I'm a butterfly!"

With a gentle movement,

he was gliding through the air,

happiness surrounded him,

the scents of the flowers everywhere.

There was so much to see,

from high up here looking down,

he flew, glided, and dipped,

taking in the beautiful colours all around.

So much to explore,

so much to do,

Harry took a deep breath,

and upwards he flew!

The other butterflies, fluttering past,

with their colours bright and lovely,

made Harry wonder about his wings,

and the colour he would be.

He tried to see himself in a pond,

but the water was too murky.

He tried to look in a puddle,

but it was too muddy and dirty.

Finally, Harry saw a greenhouse in a nearby garden,

perfect! He thought, flying over to study his reflection.

But Harry was confused, he could not see himself,

but a pink butterfly instead,

fluttering by the shelf,

she copied his every move,

it was really quite annoying,

flying closer and closer the same as Harry,

until it finally dawned on him.

Harry had realised, with a bit of a shock,

the pink butterfly staring back at him,

was him after all,

another butterfly it was not.

Harry lost flight and floated to the ground,
not knowing how to feel,
or how he would sound.
Harry curled his wings behind him,
sadness filled up inside.
Pink was not his colour,
he suddenly could not fly,
he felt his wings were not his own,
he didn't know what to do,
when a passing ladybird said "Hello"
Harry said it too.
His voice wasn't what he'd imagined,
but light and airy instead.
When the ladybird asked him his name,
he simply hung his head.
This isn't right,
there's been a mistake,
Harry thought as he walked instead of flew.
He hoped to find somebody who would help
him know what to do.

As Harry walked, with his wings tucked behind,
three other butterflies noticed him,
wondering why he was walking,
"Hey!" One called out; this one was a brilliant blue.
"How come you're walking? Are your wings hurt?" He asked.
Harry shook his head, if only they knew.
Curious, the other butterflies landed next to him.
"What's your name?" One asked.
"Harry." He replied.
"What?!" He mocked with an unfriendly grin.
They laughed at him before they flew away,
saying he had slept too long and forgotten his own name.
Harry's tears slipped down his face,
he felt so very sad,
he hadn't even noticed the black and white butterfly stay behind to catch up to his pace.

"I know how you feel." The butterfly said,

his deep voice, kind and caring.

Harry was in shock,

how could he? He looked amazing!

"I DO!" The butterfly insisted,

resting on a flower.

"I never spoke of it before, but MY real name is Amber!

I dreamed of pink wings and a soft voice,

I thought we'd become what we dreamed,

I thought that it was a choice."

After that, Harry and Amber became friends,
they understood each other,
they found they liked to sing, and their
voices sounded good together.
They continued to travel by foot,
then one day they heard crying behind a
blackberry bush,
so, Harry and Amber took a look.
They found a lovely brown butterfly there,
hiding.
"What's wrong?" They asked, wanting to
help where they can.
"It's kind of you to ask, but I don't think you
will understand."
Harry and Amber looked at each other,
then sat down and held the butterfly's hand.
"Maybe we will, maybe we wont,
but we can listen." Amber told them kindly.
"Well, it's hard to explain." The butterfly
began.

"I feel so out of place, like something's gone wrong or there's been a mistake.

You see, I love the colours. ALL of them, they represent me so wonderfully,

I used to look up at the sky,

dreaming of all the colours I would see, colours that make me happy.

Then I look at my wings and it just doesn't feel like me."

"We understand." They told the butterfly.

"We feel the same."

"You do?"

"Yes." Harry said. "It's true."

"What is your name?" Amber asked.

"Alex." The butterfly said.

"That's lovely!" Amber cried,

"It can be a boy's name or a girl's name instead."

"Exactly!" Alex cried "That's why I like it so much, I wanted my wings to show that too, but instead, I feel out of touch."

The three friends stayed together,
walking through the long grass,
they talked to each other,
feeling like they were understood at last.
Late that afternoon, the friends all heard a
loud buzzing,
A bee had come to rest with them,
curious why they were all walking.
"Hello! My, what a strange sight. Are you all
ok?"
The bee was concerned for them, ready to
help them on their way.
"I'm Harry and I don't want to talk, fly or
sing."
"What's wrong with you Harry?"
The bee exclaimed.
"Everything!"
"You see, we don't feel right in our own
wings, they're not the right colour." Alex
joined in.
"Well, my friends, what colour do you want
to be?" The bee asked.

"I want to be pink!" Amber cried.

"I want to be red!" Said Harry.

"I want to be both!" Shouted Alex.

"I see." Said the bee.

"Come with me."

The three friends followed the bee, wondering where they were going.

They walked towards a large stone with a crack running through it, realising it was an opening.

One by one they squeezed through, unsure what they would find, but as they emerged, they were amazed at what was on the other side.

All colours of the rainbow filled this wonderful space, butterflies of every colour, size and shape.

They laughed, whooped, and danced and flew and chased.

In the midst of it all was a friendly looking spider, large and hairy and working hard to spin her creation of colour.

"This is Susie." Said the bee pointing to the spider.

"She fixes wings when they get broken or are the wrong colour."

"She does?!" Alex cried, "Will she help us too?"

The bee nodded and smiled, watching the trio bloom,

into smiles and laughter that wasn't there before,

the small feeling of hope they had,

now growing into more.

The butterflies hurried over,

their faces alight with excitement,

asking Susie if she could help with their predicament.

"Of course, my dears." She agreed with a smile.

"Now which colour is YOUR silk?"

She asked, pointing to her piles.

Harry was first, he had chosen red and black.
He waited patiently while she spun,
watching his beautiful wings being created
as Susie begun.
Grateful for the friends he had met and the
kindness they had shown.
Harry slipped on his wings as soon as they
were done.
Then, with a gentle movement, he was
gliding through the air,
happiness surrounded him,
the scents of the flowers everywhere.
There was so much to see from high up here
looking down,
he flew, glided, and dipped, high and proud,
taking in the beautiful colours all around.

So much to explore,
so much to do,
Harry took a deep breath and upwards he
flew!

If YOU were a butterfly, what would be your colours?

What made you choose those colours?

What do they mean to you?

A note to parents/ carers and teachers:

I wrote this book as a gentle introduction to the conversation of transgender and non-binary for children and their parents/ caregivers and teachers.

Often when children are young, they may lack the communication tools to explain how they feel over the confusion of their own bodies, trying to conform to a stereotype and pushing down feelings they don't understand, dealing with body dysphoria and low self esteem which grows as they do, cementing mental health issues, unfortunately leading to more serious issues.

Sometimes from the simplest of conversations, the biggest of revelations are born.

I wanted to create a book that simply shows how we can feel different inside, that we may not be the only ones feeling this way and that we can talk about our feelings, that it is ok to show how we feel on the inside and that there are people that can help and accept us for who we really are; this acceptance should start young, so our children can grow feeling connected to who they are at a young age, growing in confidence and feeling proud of themselves.

Young minds create acceptance and the younger we teach them to love themselves and to be who they really are, the stronger not only they will be, but our future generation, the more they will accept themselves and their friends.

Be proud to be you. Always x

Printed in Great Britain
by Amazon